Dr Luke's Casebook

CHRISTIAN FOCUS

Text by Ruth Maclean

Illustrated by Neil Pinchbeck

Printed in Singapore

© 1996 Published by Christian Focus Publications Ltd Geanies House, Tain, Ross-shire, IV20 1TW, Scotland

Designed by Hazel Scrimshire
Reprinted 1998, 1999.

Hello there,

I'm Dr Luke. You may have heard of me, as one of the books in the Bible has the same name. I was a doctor at around the time that Jesus lived. My job was helping people who were sick to get better. Jesus also helped sick people, but he had power from God to enable him to do miracles.

I was so fascinated by the wonderful acts which Jesus did (and later some of his disciples did miracles too) that I found out all I could about them and wrote a casebook, just in the way a doctor keeps records of his patients. The amazing thing is that the people Jesus healed didn't need medicine, they were healed instantly!

Doctors' notes are usually private, but you can read all about these cases here. You will find the miracles of Jesus in the Bible in the gospel of Luke and the miracles of the disciples in the book of Acts.

PERSON: *Male*

PLACE: *A synagogue in Capernaum*

PROBLEM: *An evil spirit*

DATE: *Sabbath*

NOTES:

One day Jesus was in the synagogue, teaching the people. They were listening intently to him and were amazed at the things he said. As he spoke, screaming began. A man was yelling in a loud voice at Jesus.

The people were not too pleased at this interruption. However, this poor man had an evil spirit in him- that's what made him scream. Jesus wasn't annoyed or afraid. He calmly but clearly told the spirit to leave the man. Everyone watched and wondered. As the spirit came out of the man, it threw him onto the floor in front of everyone.

Amazingly the man was not hurt and was now free from the bad spirit. The crowd who had been watching were amazed by the power and authority which Jesus had. Imagine being healed there and then in the temple without a doctor! Jesus is really wonderful. People all around are talking about him.

REF: Luke Ch4 v31-37

CASE 2

PERSON: *Simon's mother-in-law*

PLACE: *Simon's house, Capernaum*

PROBLEM: *A high fever*

DAY: *Later on the Sabbath*

NOTES:

As soon as Jesus left the synagogue he made his way to Simon's house. Simon was one of Jesus' followers. Jesus had been told that Simon's mother-in-law was at the house and that she was very ill with a high fever. She was really sick and felt so, so hot! She couldn't get up from bed.

Everyone was very concerned, especially Simon's wife, and they were relieved when they heard that Jesus was on his way. They knew he could do wonderful things. When he arrived they showed him straight to where she was lying. He was so gentle. He stood close beside her and spoke just a few words - he told the fever to leave her. It did!!

There was no doubting how well she felt - she got up right away and began serving up food. She experienced Jesus' healing power for herself. Who is he going to heal next?

REF: Luke Ch4 v38-39

PERSON	A man
PLACE	A town in Galilee
PROBLEM	Skin disease

NOTES:

Sometimes people caught a disease which affected their skin. It was very infectious and other people could catch it quite easily. It was horrible and was called leprosy.

Jesus wasn't scared of this disease and one day he met a man who had it. The man begged Jesus to heal him and to make him clean. Jesus stretched out his hand and actually *touched* the man. No-one ever *touched* someone with this skin problem! At once the man was better, his skin was perfect again *and* Jesus didn't catch the disease. Amazing!

Jesus told the man not to tell anyone what had happened, but to go and show himself to the priest and explain to him what had happened. Jesus also told him to keep the law and offer sacrifices to God, so that he could be declared clean and return to his family. What power Jesus has!

REF: Luke Ch5 v12-14

PERSON: *A man with four special friends*

PLACE: *A house full of people in Capernaum*

PROBLEM: *Paralysis*

NOTES:

Many people were eager to know what Jesus had to say. Pharisees, teachers of the law and others came from all over the area to hear him teach. Many people had crowded into this house to hear Jesus.

Four men came along carrying a makeshift blanket. Wrapped inside was their friend. He couldn't walk, but his good friends believed that Jesus could heal him. When they arrived at the house it was full and they couldn't get in. That didn't stop them - they were determined! They went up onto the flat roof, still carrying their friend and made a hole in the roof. Then they lowered him down into the house. Jesus knew that these men must have had a lot of faith. He said to the man, 'Friend your sins are forgiven'- he didn't mention anything about being healed.

This annoyed the Pharisees and teachers who were there. They thought that only God could forgive sins. Jesus was aware of what they were thinking so he said to the man, 'Get up, pick up your mat and go home' - he did! He went away praising God. Everyone was completely amazed and gave thanks to God.

<u>REF:</u> *Luke Ch5 v17-25*

CASE 5

PERSON: *Male*

PLACE: *Synagogue*

PROBLEM: *Paralysed right hand*

DAY: *Sabbath*

NOTES:

It was the Sabbath and Jesus was in the synagogue teaching. There was a man there who had a paralysed right hand- he couldn't use it. Life would have been quite awkward for him. Also in the synagogue were many Pharisees and teachers of the law. They wondered if Jesus would heal someone on the Sabbath. They wanted to catch him doing something they considered to be wrong. Jesus knew what they were thinking.

Jesus told the man to go and stand up in front of everyone. He asked the people, 'Is it right to do good or evil on the Sabbath, save a life or let it die?' Then he told the man to stretch out his hand. When he did, it was completely healed. No operations, no bandages, no plaster. How amazed and delighted the man was. Sadly, the teachers were furious and they began to discuss what they could do to Jesus. How could they wish to hurt him?

REF: Luke 6 v6-11

PERSON: *Servant of a Roman Officer*

PLACE: *Capernaum*

PROBLEM: *Very sick and close to death*

NOTES:

Living in Capernaum was a good Roman officer. This man had a servant who was very special to him. The servant had become seriously ill and it looked like he might die. When the officer heard about Jesus, he sent some Jewish elders to ask if he would come and heal his servant. When Jesus received the message he went with them towards the house.

As they made their way along, they were met by friends of the officer. They had another message for Jesus. The Roman officer wanted Jesus to know that he felt unworthy to have Jesus come to his house or even to meet him - that was why he hadn't come himself. However he believed that Jesus had power and authority to heal his servant. This time it was Jesus who was surprised, by the faith of the Roman officer.

When the messengers returned, they found the servant was well again! Jesus' power was so great, he could even heal from a distance. What a wonderful person he is.

REF: *Luke Ch7 v1-10*

PERSON: _A widow's only son_

PLACE: _Nain_

PROBLEM: _Death_

NOTES:

This was a very sad occasion. A lady whose husband had already died and who only had one son now found her son was dead. When it was time for his funeral, the poor woman was very upset and was crying as she walked along with others who were mourning.

Jesus saw this crowd and went towards it. He felt very sorry for this lady and told her not to cry. Then he went over to where the son was and told him to get up! The man who had been dead, sat up and began to talk. This really seemed like the impossible - Jesus had brought someone back to life from the dead! No doctor could do that. Everyone who saw this was absolutely amazed and gave glory to God.

There must have been much rejoicing in the widow's house and town that night. The news of Jesus' power was spreading all around the area.

REF: _Luke Ch7 v11-17_

CASE 8

PERSON: *A man*

PLACE: *Area of Gergesa*

PROBLEM: *Demons*

NOTES:

Jesus and his disciples sailed from Galilee over to an area called Gergesa. As soon as they arrived, a strange man approached them. This man had quite a history. For many years he had lived amongst the tombs and acted very oddly. Sometimes he ran around like a wild animal. He did these things because demons lived inside him and he couldn't control his own actions.

He came to Jesus and begged him not to punish him. Jesus commanded the evil spirit to come out of the man. Then another strange thing happpened - the spirits went into a herd of pigs nearby. The pigs ran over the cliff and into the water where they drowned.

The men who cared for the pigs got such a shock that they ran away. They told everyone what had happened. Sadly the people didn't really understand and were frightened, so they asked Jesus to leave their area.

The man who had been healed wanted to go with the disciples, but Jesus told him to stay, so that he could tell others about what God had done in his life. Maybe that would help them not to be afraid.

REF: Luke Ch8 v26-39

PERSON: *A woman*

PLACE: *Street area near Lake Galilee*

PROBLEM   *Bleeding*

NOTES:

Jesus was on his way to the house of a man called Jarius. There were crowds of people all around. Amongst them was a lady who had been ill for twelve years. She desperately wanted to be well. She'd gone to many different doctors and had spent a lot of money, but nothing had made her well.

She came up behind Jesus and touched his cloak - she was healed immediately! At that moment Jesus asked who had touched him. Peter said, 'There's such a crowd, people are pushing all around you.' Jesus insisted that someone had touched him as he had felt power go from him.

Just a touch, but Jesus felt it. The poor woman realised that she had to speak up, so she came forward. She was shaking with fear. She bowed down and explained her illness to Jesus. What faith she must have had. Jesus told her to go in peace because her faith had made her well.

Quite incredible! A touch from the Master without him being told about the problem, and another healing had taken place.

REF: Luke Ch8 v43-48

PERSON: *Jarius' daughter*

PLACE: *Jarius' house*

PROBLEM: *Unknown illness*

NOTE:

Jairus had a daughter who was only twelve years old. She was so ill that people thought she was going to die. Jarius was an offical in the synagogue and he had gone to Jesus to ask him to come and heal her. On the way they were delayed by the incident with the lady in the previous case.

As Jesus made his way towards her house, someone came along to say it was too late - don't bother Jesus - the girl had died. Jarius must have been really upset. Jesus told him not to be frightened, but to believe and all would be well. They went towards the house where everyone was crying and upset because of what had happened.

Jesus only let Peter, John, and James go into the room with him and the parents. When he saw her Jesus said, ' She's only sleeping.' He took her by the hand and told her to get up, and immediately she did. Jesus told them to give her some food, but not to tell anyone what had happened. Her parents must have been delighted!

REF: Luke Ch8 v40-56

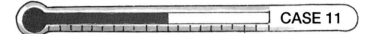

PERSON: *A boy*

PLACE: *The Mountainside*

PROBLEM: *Fits like epilepsy*

NOTE:

Jesus had been up on a mountain praying. When he came down, a large crowd was waiting for him. One man in the crowd was desperate to speak to Jesus. He only had one child, a son, and something was wrong with him. He would loose control of himself, as if in a fit and would shout and foam at the mouth.

The father had asked Jesus' followers to help but they couldn't. The man called out from the crowd to Jesus and told him the problem. Jesus asked for the boy to be brought to him. As he made his way towards Jesus, the boy fell to the ground and went into a fit. Jesus commanded the evil spirit to leave the boy. Immediately, the boy was healed and he went back to his father. Everyone was amazed at God's power. It's quite incredible!

Ref: Luke Ch9 v37-43

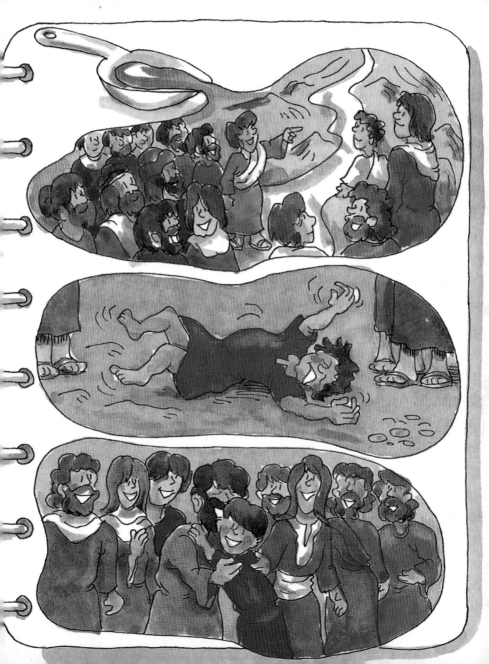

PERSON: *A woman*

PLACE: *A synagogue*

PROBLEM: *Bent over, unable to stand*

DAY: *Sabbath*

NOTE:

Jesus was often to be found teaching in the synagogue on the Sabbath. This time there was a lady there who was bent over and who couldn't straighten up. She had been like that for 18 years! Imagine not being able to stand up straight for all that time. It must have been very difficult to do anything properly or to see things clearly. Anyway, Jesus called to her, 'You're free from your sickness.' He laid his hands on her and at once she was able to straighten up. Right away she started to praise God for what had happened. I wonder what she did next? Now that she was no longer bent over, life would be quite different for her.

Once again some of the leaders were cross that Jesus had healed someone on the Sabbath. However, Jesus pointed out that animals are watered every day, even on the Sabbath, so why shouldn't this lady be freed from her sickness? The men who argued were ashamed when they heard this, but others rejoiced because of the wonders he did.

Ref: Luke Ch13 v10-17

PERSON: *A Man*

PLACE: *The home of a Pharisee*

PROBLEM: *Dropsy- a swelling of the arms and legs*

DAY :   *Sabbath*

NOTES:

While Jesus was having a meal at the house of an important Pharisee, a man came to him. His arms and legs were badly swollen. His condition was called dropsy. It was very unpleasant.

Jesus asked the officials around him if the law allowed healing on the Sabbath or not (remembering other times when there had been arguments over this). They wouldn't say! However, Jesus took the man, healed him and sent him on his way.

Ref: Luke Ch14 v1-4

PERSONS: *Ten men*

PLACE: *Small village near Jerusalem*

PROBLEM: *Skin disease*

NOTES:

Do you remember the case of the man with the skin disease? Well, here is another story about the same illness. This time there were 10 men involved. They lived outside the town because the disease spread so easily.

They saw Jesus from a distance and called out to him, asking him to take pity on them. Jesus simply told them to go and let the priest examine them - he said nothing about medicine, healing or washing themselves. On the way to the priest they discovered that they were healed, as their skin was now clean.

Sadly, only one of these men came running back to Jesus to thank him for healing him, and to praise God for his power.

Ref: *Luke Ch17 v11-19*

PERSON: *A beggar*

PLACE: *Roadside near Jericho*

PROBLEM: *Blindness*

NOTES:

As Jesus approached Jericho, a blind beggar was sitting by the road-side. The man was aware of a crowd passing by, although he couldn't see them. He wanted to know what was going on. Someone told him that Jesus of Nazareth was nearby.

When he heard who it was, the blind man called out, 'Jesus, take pity on me.' The people nearby told the man to be quiet, but that made him call out all the more. Jesus heard him call and stopped. He asked for the blind man to be brought to him. When he got close to Jesus, Jesus asked him what he wanted. The blind man replied that he would like to be able to see again. Jesus said, ' Your faith has healed you.' At once the man was able to see. He followed Jesus and gave thanks to God.

Ref: Luke Ch18 v35-43

PERSON: *High Priest's slave*

PLACE: *Mount of Olives*

PROBLEM: *Severed right ear*

NOTES:
Jesus had been praying at the Mount of Olives. After this he spent some time speaking to his disciples. As he spoke, Judas, one of the disciples, arrived with a crowd of people.

He approached Jesus to kiss him. The rest of Jesus' followers realised what was happening and asked him if they should use their swords. Jesus didn't want them to, but one of them had already lifted his sword and had hit the High Priest's servant, cutting off his right ear. Jesus said, 'Stop!' and he touched the man and healed him. An ear replaced without surgery or medical treatment!

Once again Jesus displayed his miraculous healing power.

Ref: *Luke Ch22 v47-51*

PERSON: *A Man*

PLACE: *Near the Temple*

PROBLEM: *Lameness*

TIME: *3 o'clock in the afternoon*

NOTES:
One afternoon Peter and John went up to the Temple to pray. On the way they came to a place called the Beautiful Gate. Sitting there, was a lame man. He had been unable to walk all his life. He was carried there every day to beg from the people going in to the Temple.

He begged Peter and John to give him money, but they explained to him that they had none. However, they told him that they could give him something else. Peter ordered him, in the name of Jesus, to get up and to start walking. Peter helped him to his feet and immediately his feet and ankles became strong. He jumped up and walked into the Temple, leaping and praising God. The people who saw him were amazed at this miracle.

Ref: *Acts Ch3 v1-10*

PERSON: *Aeneas*

PLACE: *Lydda*

PROBLEM: *Paralysis*

NOTES:

Peter travelled around many places telling people about Jesus. On one occasion he went to visit the people who lived in a place called Lydda. There he met Aeneas who hadn't been out of his bed for eight years because he was paralysed.

Peter said to him, 'Jesus makes you better, get up!' Aeneas got out of his bed right away. All the people living in the area saw this and they turned and believed in Jesus.

Even after his death, Jesus was still at work through his disciples.

Ref: *Acts Ch9 v32-35*

CASE 19

PERSON: *Tabitha, also called Dorcas*

PLACE: *Joppa*

PROBLEM: *Unknown illness*

NOTES:

A lady called Dorcas lived in Joppa. She was very kind and did many good things to help the poor. She had become ill and it seemed as if she was dead. She had been put into an upstairs room. The believers sent a message to Peter to see if he would come quickly and do something to help. Joppa wasn't far from where Peter was, in Lydda.

By the time Peter arrived everyone was upset. He put everyone out of the room, knelt down by Dorcas and prayed. Then he told her to get up. Her eyes opened and she was able to get out of bed - she was alive!

The news spread about this miracle and as a result many people believed in Jesus.

Ref: *Acts Ch9 v36 - 43*

Have you ever been ill or known someone who has been sick? You could make a medical record here in my files.

PERSON:
_____

ADDRESS:
_____

AGE:
_____

PROBLEM:
_____

DOCTOR'S NAME:
_____

MEDICINE TO BE TAKEN:
_____

NOTES:
_____

Jesus' power to heal was quite incredible and many people believed in him because of what they saw. Today we can't see Jesus in the way that people did in Bible times, but he still has the power to forgive sin and to heal the sick. You could help someone who is ill by asking Jesus to make them better.

These cases are only some of the miracles we read about in the Bible. Many other miracles are mentioned too. I was fascinated to learn that the Old Testament part of the Bible records some amazing stories of healing.

I carried out some research and have added these details to my files. This shows that God has always had the power to heal people.

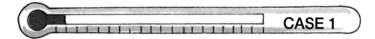

Old Testament Files:

PERSON: *Naaman, Army Commander*

PLACE: *River Jordan*

PROBLEM: *Leprosy*

NOTES:

Naaman was a very important man in the army, but he had a problem - he had leprosy. His young servant girl told him about a prophet in Samaria who could help him. Naaman asked for permission from the king to go there to see him.

First of all he went to see the King of Israel, but he could not cure him. Then Elisha, the prophet of God, heard about Naaman and sent for him.

Naaman went to Elisha and was given a strange message - 'Go and wash in the River Jordan seven times, and you will be healed.'

This made Naaman angry - why should he go and wash in that muddy river? Eventually his servants persuaded him to give it a try. He dipped himself in the water seven times as he'd been told. When he came out the last time, his skin was totally clear from the horrible disease. Because he obeyed Elisha, God had miraculously healed him. What a mighty God he is!

<u>REF:</u>   *2 Kings Ch 5v 1-14*

PERSON: *Many people*

PLACE: *Around Edom*

PROBLEM: *Snake bites*

NOTES:

The people of Israel had been travelling around in the desert for a long time. On this occasion they were impatient about the way they were going and spoke against God. They complained about the lack of food and water.

The Lord sent snakes amongst the camp which bit the people and caused many of them to die. When they realised that they had angered God and had sinned against him, the people came to Moses and asked him to pray that God would take the snakes away.

Moses prayed and the Lord's reply was that Moses was to make a snake and put it on a pole. Anyone who was bitten was to look at this snake and they would live. This is just what happened. People were healed by looking at the snake - it was God's awesome power that healed them.

REF: Numbers Ch 21 v4-9

Who was healed where?

I am a woman, healed of a high fever in this town

I was a blind beggar on a roadside near to this place

Mediterranean Sea

Capernaum

GALILEE
Nazareth

Gergesa

Lake Galilee

A boy was brought back to life here

Nain

Ten of us were healed of a skin disease near this town

Caesarea

Aeneas was healed of paralysis here

I was freed from demons in this area

Joppa

Jericho

Lydda

A man was healed from an evil spirit in the temple here

Jerusalem

Dorcas was healed at this place

Dead Sea

Can you match the patient to the place?